Return to Michael

Return to Michael

✦

A Transgender Story

Michael Brinkle

iUniverse, Inc.
New York Lincoln Shanghai

Return to Michael
A Transgender Story

iUniverse books may be ordered through booksellers or by contacting:

iUniverse
2021 Pine Lake Road, Suite 100
Lincoln, NE 68512
www.iuniverse.com
1-800-Authors (1-800-288-4677)

The views expressed in this work are solely those of the author and do not necessarily reflect the views of the publisher, and the publisher hereby disclaims any responsibility for them.

ISBN-13: 978-0-595-39969-7 (pbk)
ISBN-13: 978-0-595-84357-2 (ebk)
ISBN-10: 0-595-39969-X (pbk)
ISBN-10: 0-595-84357-3 (ebk)

Printed in the United States of America

Contents

Introduction

I was born and raised in the time of the hippies and free love. Elvis, The Beatles, The Mamas and The Papas, and The Supremes were the rage of many. I witnessed the assassination of President Kennedy and the first moon landing. On television, I Love Lucy, Ed Sullivan, The Honeymooners, and movies like King Kong and Tarzan were showing.

So why would a young boy named Michael, born in 1951, who was abandoned to a Children's Home at 3 years of age, and was sexually abused get a sex change at 18 to become Michelle, sow her wild oats for 10 years as a stripper and prostitute, and decide to return to Michael at 29 years old once again.

Travel along with me as I relive my experiences with you, including all the highs and lows of my life. Come share with me in my memories, have some laughs, and at the same time shed a few tears. These are my memories.

Preface

In my mind, I remember it was a beautiful spring day in Memphis. The sky was clear. The sun was bright. Oh, how I loved Mama and Sis. The three of us were all together. There was so much love for them in my heart. Funny though, I can't recall Daddy in my mind, but at the time, it didn't really matter. After all, it was just me and the girls in my life.

Mama and Sis looked just alike. I loved playing with Mama's long brunette hair and looking into her dark brown eyes. She was so beautiful. Nothing could be better. I loved them, and I was the love of their lives, or so I thought.

1

"We're going for a drive out in the country," Mama said. My sister and I were so excited! I was three and she was five. When we pulled into an estate of big buildings, it was strange! What is this I thought? Mama said, "Stay in the car for a few minutes." We finally went in after Mama came back and got us out of the car. "You have to stay here," she said. Sis and I were really frightened by now.

"I don't understand. Why do we have to stay here," I asked.

"You just do. I have to go now. They are going to take care of you now," she said.

I wouldn't remember my father even if he were sitting next to me right now. I do remember throwing the biggest temper tantrum ever because Mama left us at the Baptist Children's Home in Memphis, Tennessee. A scar in my mind forever!

My sister and I were put in the little children's building for kids one through six years of age. I drew close to Mama Maude Kilebrew, a house-mother there. She was in her sixty's and had long white hair rolled up in a bun, except at night when she would let it down. I remember that I loved to play with her hair. I didn't draw close to the Raisin Bran cereal they shoved down our throats every morning.

We learned to adapt. After all, there were many other kids to play with. Mama Maude even let me sleep with her. She was like a grandmother I never knew. We would go downtown shopping, getting candy and nuts every so often. One time the nuts came with worms (shades of the Raisin Bran).

On the playground one day a bug hit my ear. I screamed to a house-mother, "A bug flew into my ear!" Acting concerned, she said, "Are you sure?"

"Yes, it's in there, look and see," I cried.

"Well," she said, "it flew out the other ear, because it's not in this one!"

Brother Butler ran a tight ship at the Home. One day, Mama Maude let me put on one of her dresses. I was thrilled. She put lipstick on me and I bolted out into the yard and paraded around the grounds, feeling full of glee as most kids would. Brother Butler caught me, and I'll never forget that paddling! As far as he was concerned, I was a sinner and was going to burn in hell for wearing women's clothes. He said that I had better never, ever do that again! At that age and point in my life though, if you told me not to do something and I would want to do it more!

We went to church every Wednesday evening and Sundays. Those sermons had me so scared I went down the aisle three different times to be saved, so I wouldn't burn in hell. I wanted to be baptized, but every time they said, "You're too young, boy. Go back to your seat!" I just knew I was going to burn in hell before I was old enough to get baptized. I did enjoy Vacation Bible School. We learned about Jesus and Bible stories and got great treats.

My future adoptive mother started coming to the Baptist Children's Home to find a child to call her own, as many other couples did. I felt like a ping-pong ball at times. Being parentless at three, I craved love and attention.

One Sunday afternoon, a housemother said, "Come on, Butch, you have visitors." I am not sure where that nickname came from but I have never been a fan of it! When I walked into the room, low and behold, there sat three couples waiting to see me! Being shy, I didn't know who to go to. My future adoptive mother was wearing a neck brace because of a traffic accident, so naturally, that drew me to her. I suspect it might have been a ploy to get me to draw to her. She knew other people were interested in me also. When she found out I had a sister, Mother was interested in adopting both of us. Sis has held that against me until this day!

We were allowed to go home with them on weekends. Monday through Friday, though, we had to stay at the Children's Home. What a tug of war on your emotions! It seemed like we lived in two different worlds.

My real mother was manic-depressive, I later found out, and couldn't take care of us. Sis inherited more of it than I did. My adoptive mother used to say Sis was in the room 'sulking'. Back then the medical field just thought you were 'crazy' when you had this disease.

I don't blame Mom for putting us in the Baptist Children's Home. At least she didn't abort us or drown us, as is so common today. She cared enough to give us life and hoped the best for us.

As the years went by, we were showered with gifts by our future adoptive parents. We had many happy holidays on the weekends. Many groups brought gifts of fruit and nuts to all the children at the home on Christmas. We really cherished those times!

Pictures of Sis and I were used on the Baptist Children's Home's flyers to help promote their donations for their three Children's Homes across the state of Tennessee.

I'm certainly grateful for the homes housing and feeding us kids. The alternative could have been similar to a Charles Dickens novel about the kids orphaned on the streets.

My adoptive parents really did love us kids. Mom would turn out all the lights and we would play 'Kitty Cat,' although she didn't like real cats at all. She would meow while Sis and I would crawl around on the floor on our hands and knees to look for her. When we came close to her she would jump out and scare us.

At other times, she would ask me to be her little helper. I loved washing the Bel-Air Chevy. One time, though, as I was on the hood and had the car all soapy, I slipped down and my arm caught the hood ornament. Blood and soap were gushing everywhere.

"Mom! Mom! Come get me down," I yelled.

"What is it Butch? I'm busy now," she yelled back.

"I'm stuck on the hood of the car," I yelled.

Well, she finally came out the side door and started screaming, "Get in the car! We're going to the hospital!" My arm was torn open, and it almost hit a main artery. It took 14 stitches. The same arm was broken at the Children's Home a few years earlier. I was swinging high on the swing set when one of the other kids dared me to jump and I did.

Dad made a go-cart from parts of a lawn mower. I really felt like I was an adult driving it on the street. Although one day he gave me too big of a push on my bike, without training wheels and I skidded off the driveway onto the sidewalk scraping the whole side of my body. I remember being mad at him a long while.

They really tried hard to be good parents and we were so thankful to be with them away from the Children's Home. Dad raised beagle puppies, so we always had pets. One night for supper, Mom made a big dish of spaghetti. She had all our plates fixed when this pesky fly landed right in my spaghetti! She swore she gave me a new plate in the kitchen, but I'm still not so sure to this day.

2

"Come on, you have to get packed, lets go," Mama Maude yelled!

"Go where," I asked.

"You're going to the big boys building."

"But I want to stay here with you Mama Maude," I cried.

"I'll come and see you, but you have to go! You're six years old now, let's go!" My sister was already at the 'big girls building', and I really missed her.

One day I snuck over to see her. "What are you doing here? You're going to get me in trouble," she yelled!

"But, Sis, it's me, your brother!"

"You go back to your building or you'll get me in trouble." I left in tears. I was so crushed. I loved her so much; I really thought she would be glad to see me.

The sexual abuse by the older boys at the home was repressed until the early 1990's when I saw an Oprah Winfrey show on repressed memory. I realized then that the older boys were doing more than just 'playing' and 'wrestling' with me between the beds. They had me lie on my stomach and be still for a while, with my underwear pulled down. It all came back like a bolt of lightening. I had convinced myself over the years they simply couldn't be doing that. *Not that*!

That also explains why I would get up during the night and draw pictures by the light of the hallway. Mama Maude taught me some artistic skills, but I was never as good as she was. The abuse went on for years and drawing got my mind off of it.

We also had fun playing softball and games. Of course we had work to do too, helping with the chickens and crops (shades of "Little Orphan Annie"). Mama Smith was a nice house Mom at the big boys building. I'll never forget those 'Ivory Soap baths'. She had to persuade me to get undressed at times, I was so shy.

But Mama Crouch was something else! One night a few of us boys ran the halls, up and down the stairs playing all night. She never came out of her room and we really thought we had gotten away with something. Early the next morning we were proven wrong. 'Old Crouch the Grouch' as we called her, got her victory by throwing back our covers, flipping us over while we were sleeping and letting the licks fly with that old wooden paddleboard. OUCH!! I can still remember the pain!

I was on all the other boys' black list one Saturday afternoon. King Kong was on the late show Friday night. Mama Smith said it was way too late for us to stay up and watch it. Our begging and pleading didn't do any good either.

The television station then always ran the same Friday night movie the next afternoon. So I spoke up and said, "Let's watch it tomorrow. It will be on then." Everybody was in agreement.

But this Saturday they didn't run it. My payback was when I was shown a "spider web" in an evergreen tree with my name in it. They said, "If ever a spider weaves someone's name in her web its sure death!"

I started to reach up and touch it. "Don't ever touch a spider web because if you do, it is instant death," they stated in a scary voice. I jerked my hand back. "I don't want to die," I cried.

For years, I was waiting and wondering how I was going to die, that was until I saw many other "spider webs" with other people's names on them in a store one day.

3

It was Christmas time at my future adoptive parents' house. We were there for the weekend. One of the gifts was for Sis and me. It was a Snow White doll and the Seven Dwarfs! I threw my second biggest tantrum ever when I found out Snow White wasn't for me, but the Seven Dwarfs were. A short time later I had a little male doll of my own.

I can't say at what age I realized I was supposed to be a girl, not a boy, but the sexual abuse thrust me in that direction, I'm sure. I was turned into a woman by quite a few incidents in my life.

Learning about sex the wrong way can damage your life. My adoptive parents had a full length mirror on their bedroom door. With their door cracked, I could see their bed from my bedroom. During some sleepless nights, I saw things I really wish I hadn't seen and things a young boy shouldn't have seen. No wonder I had a hard time dealing with sex later on.

When I stumbled upon Dad's pornography in my early teens, it started making sense in my mind how to get a fathers love that I never had received—sex with women! Men loved you if they could have sex with you. No wonder I hadn't received my father's love! If only I was a girl, he would surely have loved me then. If only they had family counseling in the 1950's, things may have turned out very different.

My adoptive mother let me play with her jewelry all the time. As I got older I started dressing up in her clothes and shoes when no one was around. Instead of wanting to be with Marilyn Monroe or the other movie stars, I wanted to be them!! I imitated them, sang and danced like them. "Why couldn't I have been a girl?" I repeated this to myself over and over again. Something was wrong, I just didn't understand what.

In my early formative years, my real father left us, as you know, so I had no role model to follow. I felt that there must have been something wrong with me for him to have left us! These thoughts played over and over again in my mind. I started desiring men to fill that void in my teen years and getting them. I loved fixing and playing with the hair on the neighbors' dolls when I babysat them. I wanted to become a hairdresser someday.

Sis and I were finally legally adopted by the time I was nine years old. No more Monday through Friday's at the Baptist Children's Home! I only returned there one more time in my life. I'll tell you more about that later. My real Mama died of lung cancer at forty-three, shortly after our adoption. We saw her two times between three and nine years of age. She wasn't well. I shied up again at seeing her so it wasn't much of a visit. I think she felt guilty about leaving us at the Children's Home. My adoptive mother wouldn't even take us to her funeral, for whatever reason. I don't even have a picture of her or my father.

More abuse happened in cub scouts and on vacations, so these kinds of things started to seem "normal" to me. I thought that I must be a woman because men crave me. Weekend camping trips turned into abuse by some of the older scouts who wanted me to sleep in their tents. Of course, that filled the missing fatherly love I had so desperately needed! In fact, I started looking for manly love. One of the neighborhood boys and I had sleepovers on Friday nights and things eventually developed into after school "dates". He was able to leave all that behind him and get married and later have children. I was turned into more of a woman by the affair.

I put on Sis' makeup and loved to watch her fix her hair. *Why couldn't I be doing that? Why wasn't I born a girl?* After school I would clomp around in Mother's high heels and fill one of her busty bras with socks and put it on. Later on, I was befriended by a young lad at the Catholic school I went to for a year. He showed me a book by Christine Jorgensen. She was in the military, but later on had a sex change, one of the first. I was fascinated and thrilled. This was what I wanted. I knew I wasn't gay, how could I be when I wanted to be a woman?

John, my friend from catholic high school and another friend would come over to my house after school. We would put on makeup and fix our hair like the Supremes! Then we would sing and dance like them. John was Dianna, Hugh was Flo, and I was Mary. Ooooh, Ooooh, Baby Love, Oh Baby Love!!!

During my middle teens, Sis left home at eighteen and was married. She left a year earlier, but my parents made her come back home. They just never really got along together. We visited a few times, but I realized later that the love was not there for me. She looked up my real dad and found him, but couldn't even get out of the car to go and talk to him. Her husband went to get him out of the house. Dad came out to the car window, but Sis couldn't even roll it down and talk to him.

I never had the desire to find him because I knew I would have nothing but feelings of extreme anger towards him for what he did to us. I realize now he may have had his own set of problems as we all do, but it's still hard. People with normal families should be so thankful for what they have!

I think Sis rejected me for loving my adoptive parents. I also believe she may have blamed me for the breakup of our first family. After three children, she divorced and married an older man. She was also looking for that "father figure" in her life.

Sis and my adoptive mother were always pulling me in a tug of war vying for my love. I was torn between two loves. My adoptive mother was a bit of a dictator. It was her way or the highway. Sis took the highway at eighteen and so did I, which is where life gets far more interesting for me!

4

By the time I was seventeen, I was dating a few girls. I didn't know what to do though, because how could I marry them when I wanted to be them? I've regretted hurting a close girlfriend of mine at the time. I'm sure she was leaning toward love and marriage, but I couldn't tell her I wanted to be a girl. I was <u>so</u> confused. We went to dances together and had great fun!

I met a guy named Lance and started dating him when I left Catholic high school and was transferred to White Station High School. We were dating at least in my eyes. He only had one friend, but I grew infatuated with him.

It's so difficult being a teenager, with your hormones racing. You want to be liked and loved, and you want to love. You also want to be understood by your parents and your peers. Can you change or can you change the world? Lance had a beautiful smile and face, not to mention those hazel eyes, and, oh, his dishwater blond hair. How we ache over those teenage crushes. I joined Lance and his friend for lunch period. His other friend drifted away so it was just the two of us. I wondered if he felt the way I did. He acted so nice toward me. Maybe he just felt sorry for me.

One day, Lance invited me to a drive-in movie. "I'll drive and pick you up," I said all giddishly. "One Million Years B.C." was playing with Raquel Welch. We had a great time. Many more movies followed.

We are really dating I thought. One night at the drive-in, it was so cold and Lance said, "Why don't you move over closer to me and get warm??"

This is it! I thought. I inched over a little but stopped. I tried again but couldn't go any farther. Why, I don't know. Was that an invitation or not?

Nothing ever happened then or again after that night. He also rejected me later. He wouldn't have anything to do with me either. I went to his house looking for him, even peering in the windows. But, no, Lance wouldn't have anything to do with me. At school, he ignored me.

What happened? In my mind I just knew that this happened because I wasn't a girl. So I vowed then I would get him when I had my change! I loved him so much. Or was it just after all a childish crush?

I finally told my parents I thought I was gay. When I told them I had relations with men, they hit the ceiling. "You can't be. What do you mean? What's going on? Haven't you been doing it with girls," Mom screamed. Dad was silent and let Mom handle it.

"No, I haven't. I couldn't," I said.

Looking for sympathy, one afternoon before they got home from work I took a whole bottle of Sleepeze sleeping aid. I didn't think it would kill me, but I timed it so they would find me. Boy was I high! They found me laying sprawled out on the bed, one arm hanging over the side with the empty bottle and top laying in the floor. I think I might have been a bit overdramatic. They got me dressed and said they were going to get me some help. *It's working*, I thought.

Much to my surprise when the elevator door opened at the Baptist Hospital, we were in the psychiatric ward! I was in there two weeks, and some of those people really were_ crazy. Some were counting invisible things, others laughing at nothing. I did some fast-talking with the psychiatrist, let me tell you. "I'm really not gay after all!! I didn't mean to take those pills. I won't do any of this again," I cried. I can't imagine what would have happened if I had told them I wanted to be a girl! Maybe they would have done shock treatments!

When I got out of the hospital, I heard they were doing some trans-gender surgery at John Hopkins Hospital in Baltimore, Maryland. The only problem was you had to wait for 2 years to go through mental evaluation. But, if I could just get to Baltimore, somehow I might be able to get my lifelong dream I wanted. Then nobody would call me gay or sissy, or make fun of me ever again. I wouldn't be gay, because I would be a woman. I wanted straight men, not gay men.

I had some money saved from working after school. In 1969 four hundred dollars was a lot of money. Mother and I had argued about me sneaking out at night. I was forever grateful to my folks for taking us out of the Children's Home, but I had to follow my own path in life. I really felt nobody ever understood me. All my life people seemed to love me if I did things their way and hated me if I didn't. So, I packed up, left a going away note on the T.V. and took a Greyhound Bus to Baltimore after I graduated from high school at age 18. I didn't tell my folks where I was going, just that I had to go.

I really made some bold chances in my life. Was I brave, determined and or just plain crazy going after my life long dream? I think it must have been the plain crazy one, because at 11, when I had to give a book report at school that I didn't prepare for, I faked illness. This has got to be a good one, I thought, to be able to stay home. The night before I told Mom I was sick. She ran and got the thermometer and stuck it in my mouth. Then she left the room. I took it out and laid it on the light bulb in my desk lamp to heat it up!! The problem was that it burst the glass. I didn't know what to do then. So I stuck it back in my mouth. When she pulled it out again she screamed, "Oh, my gosh. You'll get mercury poisoning! What happened? "It just broke," I said. I got to stay home for the mercury poisoning anyway.

It's no wonder you hate school when you are different. One bully knocked the wind out of me in junior high when he hit me in my stomach in the hallway between classes. Others made fun of my singing after the music teacher praised my voice for being a beautiful tenor. Also, in junior high, the whole class set me up with another wimp for a fight after school. I was so nervous when I walked out the door in the back of the school. Everybody was there egging us on. I thought to myself, I am no fighter! It was a good thing he wasn't either! All we did was circle around the school yard with our fists up in the air until everybody got tired of waiting for some action and left, including us!

5

Getting off the bus in Baltimore was exciting. I was in the very city that performed trans-gender surgery! I checked into a sleazy hotel, a one roomer with common baths. I already had a wig and some female clothes, so I dressed up a few times. Believe it or not, most people didn't pick up that I was a guy. I even got honks and whistles walking down the street. One evening, I came back to the hotel in drag and the night clerk asked, "Where do you think you are going?"

"To my room," I said.

"You don't have a room here," he said.

"Yes I do, its right up there," I insisted and kept going toward the stairs.

"No women are allowed in this hotel," he yelled.

I had to get into my room so I bolted up the stairs, opened the door, jerked off my wig, and jumped under the covers of the bed. He had the nerve to open my door with the passkey and yell, "No women allowed here!"

I pretended to be sleeping and said, "What's going on?"

"I saw a woman come in here, where is she?" he demanded.

"Look for yourself, there's not one in here," I said as I yawned. He was dumbfounded and left after checking the closet. He kept a close eye on me after that experience.

I moved into an apartment after that! My sister sent me a check for three hundred dollars she had borrowed to that hotel and I never received it. I realized later that the clerk had stolen it.

After moving into my new apartment, I found a job at the Pimlico Hotel, a restaurant near the racetrack. It was quite the high-class restaurant. I had gained experience by working in the House of Pancakes restaurant in Memphis. It was there, at the House of Pancakes that I went from dishwasher to host and cashier. One of the guys that bullied me there would come by and make fun of me. He used to work there and then quit, because he couldn't stand it because I got promoted and he didn't. I think the manager was gay so he favored me. Later, he tried to get me to move to Nashville to open a new House of Pancakes, but I declined.

One night that bully came in drunk, causing a scene, and ready to fight! Me being a sissy, didn't know what to do, so on instinct I bolted toward the door and pushed him out. He never came back after that. I understood then that bullies are really just cowards trying to exert their power on the weak!

I kept thinking, at this rate of pay, I'll be too old to get a sex change. Things just weren't going the way I had hoped for in Baltimore. I met Les sitting on a park bench one day. He was looking for love, but I didn't like gay sex. After all, women didn't do it that way. Besides, somebody tried it with me one time and it hurt. That was not for me! We dated, me in drag, he was my prince in shining armor, a real gentleman. He kept telling me how beautiful I was and that he was crazy about me. I felt like a schoolgirl in love for the first time. He even took me to meet his parents, in drag! I think his dad suspected something, because he reached up while we were playing pool and grabbed at my chin. I jerked away, surprised! I'm glad I shaved really close before I went there.

Les finally convinced me to have sex with him, or it was date rape, close to it anyway. He was rough, crude, and I hated it. It didn't really seem natural to me. We soon broke up after that incident.

Back at the Pimlico Hotel one evening after work, I was waiting at the bus stop. Two policemen pulled up and stopped in their cruiser. One of them said they thought they had seen me down on the 'Block'. I asked, "What is the Block?"

"It's a section of town where there are night clubs and bars. All the action is down there," they declared.

Why they told me that, I don't know. I wasn't in drag. I went down to the Block and saw so many clubs. Tourists and people were all over the place. I discovered a club off the main drag called the Inferno. Drag queens and trans-gender people worked there, along with a few real girls. I was given a job there, go-go dancing and hustling drinks and champagne. I had finally made it to *HELL* as the Baptist preacher said I would!!

Trans-genders who were half and half went from the smaller go-go bars to the strip joints after full surgery. Blazz Star, the stripper who was involved in a scandal with a U.S. Senator, owned her own club there. I eventually worked there for six months for her. She was so nice.

I met Kelly, a real girl, at the Inferno bar. She was blonde, short, and sassy! She had just ended her relationship with her boyfriend who was also a pimp. He had been abusing not only Kelly but her poodle named 'Pearl'. She said she couldn't take the abuse anymore.

"Michelle, if you move in with me, he won't come back," she said. "Plus, you can protect me from him if he does."

"Yeah, right," I said. "He's 6'2" and I'm 5'10" and a gender bender."

I did move in with her, taking another bold chance in my life. He only came back one time. Nothing happened though. I think she could have taken not only him on, but the whole world. She was famous for being gutsy and high spirited. Which I am sure was the reason she stayed in a lot of trouble. She expected any one of her friends who was close by at the time to come to her aide.

I needed to help her many times when she experienced seizures from taking to many barbiturates and other drugs. She would have withdrawal symptoms when she stopped taking them. I would place a tube of lipstick between her teeth so she wouldn't swallow her tongue. Five minutes later, the seizures would stop. It was quite the experience to go through. I received a fast education by experiencing the realities of the 'night life'.

Salomé and another transgender also named Michelle overdosed on barbiturates called 'red and blues'. Many were getting high on them. The problem was after taking a few you would forget how many you popped. Salomé would get them from a 'john' in the pharmaceutical business. She would pass them out to everyone. It was so sad. They were beautiful and were only in their early twenties.

I think many gays and trans-genders are really unhappy inside. It doesn't matter what kind of life we lead. We've already received that third strike against us at birth. Anyone hooked on the 'night life' also has their own set of problems that they are trying to mask. They get involved in it for many reasons: love, love of money, and their fifteen minutes of fame.

There was one old prostitute that had a wooden leg. She also worked at the Inferno Club. She hustled drinks and got dates too. She took the train from Philly for short periods of time to work and hustle some money. She had a husband who was disabled and a couple of kids to support. Margo would stay with some of the queens. She kept her money inside her wooden leg. Some of the queens would take her leg and hide it from her! Being feisty and not taking any bull from them, she would scream and cuss them out until they gave her leg back.

Some of the queens and trans-genders fought and argued. Many had small 'cat fights', but others really had some serious issues. One time we watched two of them boxing, just like men, in full drag!

Many of the dancers turned tricks with the Johns and I was no exception. My first trick wanted a girl and a queen at the same time. I didn't know what I was doing. So laying there with the two of them, all I did was talk for an hour. Kelly was so mad at me for talking so long. We were late for work to boot!

The back door of the 'Inferno' club was connected to the 'Gypsy's' next door. It was a good thing the door was left open all the time. Kelly and I ran and hid in their business one night when we were raided by the police! The Gypsy's didn't mind. They read our fortunes one day for us. "You and Kelly are going to have two children each," they predicted!

Kelly spoke up and said, "See you don't know anything!! Michelle's a man and she can't have any children! So there, what do you say to that?" The Gypsy's cleaned it up by saying I was going to be the father of Kelly's two children! I don't think so!

Kelly did end up pregnant though. By now you know it couldn't have been mine. The baby was by a trick, so she decided to get an abortion. I begged her not to do this. She insisted that she couldn't take care of the baby and didn't want it. Besides, the world was too wicked for a child to grow up in she argued. I did agree to go with her and help her. At this point I was worried about what could happen to her physically. It was quite an experience to go through in 1969.

Later on a Hispanic dancer gave herself an abortion with a coat hanger! She did it right in the club over the toilet too. Kelly and I couldn't believe

19

that one! She could have bled to death. An hour later, she went on stage and danced to "Me and Mrs. Jones." The whole thing is still unbelievable!

When working in the Inferno, some clients knew the story, others didn't, and some just didn't care. I worked every evening and then I started also to work early afternoons. The money came in fast and before I knew it, Kelly and I were on our way to New York. Me to get breast implants, and she was getting silicone injections to enhance her breasts. They put me in the women's ward at Yonker's Hospital for the surgery. I really felt like a woman then! Kelly stayed right by my side the whole time.

I gave up on John Hopkins Hospital because I was too busy and they evaluated you too long. A short time after my breast implants, I had a nose job to make my nose a little smaller, and I also had a little silicone in my cheeks and buttocks to fill in the curves. There was also a local doctor who gave out female hormones. All of this at just eighteen years of age!

I became friends with another trans-gender male. She had all silicone-injected breasts. That could be dangerous because I knew of a queen that was enlarging her breasts that way and the needle punctured her lung, filling it up with silicone and killing her. A so called doctor came to town every so often pumping the girls and trans-genders full of silicone. We called him 'Dr. Plastic'. He mixed the silicone in the bathtub! Rumors were going around that he used 'Turtle Wax'! No, he didn't finish us off with a buff cloth either! He was later arrested and put on trial for killing that trans-gender. Kelly was supposed to testify against him but she started getting death threats over the phone. Needless to say, she didn't testify. They eventually had to cut a lot of the silicone out of her because it became infected. The silicone didn't seem to have that effect on men for some reason.

Mae looked like a tall Ursula Andress, the move star in James Bond. I was told I looked like Ann Margaret. Mae said they were doing sex changes in Casablanca, Morocco and that she was going there to have it done. "I'm not happy with the way I am," she said.

"Me either," I told her. So we made plans to go to Morocco (shades of Humphrey Bogart and Ingrid Bergman).

Getting a passport was quite another story. Two boys with breasts, looking like two girls, with male birth certificates!! The passport agent in Washington, D.C. said no way and that we couldn't do it. We waited there for about three hours then Mae finally got disgusted and said, "Give us the 'blanking' passports or we're gonna report you! You can't stop us from going!" He did give them to us after that.

So, when I was nineteen and Mae was twenty-six, with two thousand dollars each for the surgery, we flew to Casablanca, where a French doctor was performing the surgery.

I was crushed when Doctor Bereau said I was too young at nineteen for the surgery. I started crying and begging and pleading with him, "Please, please do it!" I took out two thousand dollars in traveler's checks and showed them to him. "Please," I said again. Money talked and he agreed to perform the surgery.

The night before the surgery I masturbated as Michael for the last time. I pictured myself as a woman having sex, as I always did. We had heard the surgery done in Morocco was done so you could still have orgasms. Those performing it in America just made a hole there. Dr. Bereau formed a clitoris and vagina. The clitoris fills with blood and you climax but it's a little different from a male climax, plus you're castrated! He uses the penis to form the vaginal walls. We were in the hospital for two weeks before we hobbled out. We stayed two more weeks to rest up some more, were we ever sore!

Mae convinced me to go to a French restaurant with her. I said, "Sure, it sounds great to me!" When we arrived at the restaurant, the menu was all in French! Mae said, "Trust me, I will word for us. I eat French food all the time." That dinner was the most delicious meal I had ever eaten. I finished every bite. I begged Mae to tell me what I ate. She finally did, after more coercing. It was cow's tongue! Yuck! I was so mad at her for fooling me. If she hadn't already had a sex change, I would gladly have given her one myself after finding that out!! Finally, it was time to go back to the States as women!

6

I thought it best to call Mother and tell her now. I'd been away from home now for about a year (about time, you say!). Well, it wasn't as easy as you would think. I didn't want to hurt her or Daddy!

Six beers later and I was ready! She could not believe it. "How could you do something like that? How could you, Butch," she cried. Imagine her calling me Butch when my name was now Michelle.

"But Mother," I pleaded, "I could have died on the operating table if God didn't want me to change! So, it must be okay! I've always felt this way inside, I just couldn't tell you." Mother and Daddy wanted me to marry so they could have grandkids, but it just wasn't for me.

Believe it or not, she came to accept my decision and started considering me as a second daughter, though she still called me Butch. Dad was a little more reserved.

Mom finally said, "You better call the selective service board, they've been looking for you."

"They don't want me," I said.

"You still have to call them and register." Well, I thought, this is going to be quite a show.

I walked into the selective service office in Baltimore. "May I help you," the lady behind the desk asked.

"Yes, I'm Michael Brinkle, reporting for registration." All eyes in the office were upon me.

After the formalities, I was later informed that the Army wanted to see me *personally*. I had to report to an Army doctor for a physical to verify everything.

I made sure I wore the sexiest thing I had. When I walked in, the doctor had a big smile on his face, shook my hand, and asked, "Are you Michael?" I wanted to say, do I look like Michael, but thought I'd better be good if I wanted to get out of this trouble. So, I said yes.

"Well, you'll need to disrobe. But first, let's move over by the window so I can get a *good look* at you." I got the message quite clear. A few of his friends were also getting a good look from across the other building. So I gave it to them all!! I stripped totally naked! I was finally classified 4-F!!

7

I finally found the first love of my life, except for a couple of high school crushes that didn't like me in return. The only problem was that he was A.W.O.L from the Army, and oh, yes, had a wife and child out west.

Once I woke up one morning and grabbing the wrong tubes, I brushed my teeth with Preparation H and had a cool, minty feeling down below where the Preparation H was to go! I was starting to think my life was ending up that way also. Danny, as I'll call him, was making the rounds with the queens, gender-benders, girls, and boys! He looked just like John Travolta, the actor. He was so cute, handsome, and for me! That cute little dimple in the middle of his chin rounded him out!

To hide him from the army and to get classified as 4-F, Danny wanted me to dress him up in drag. He also worked at the Inferno club for a while. What an ugly girl, but he made money. He sold drinks and got dates!

He had just ended an affair with a queen when we moved in together. It was just like being married. After a few months he wanted me to meet his parents in Florida. Sounded great to me, so off to Florida we went, on a motorcycle that is! We stopped in North Carolina to visit his brother and a friend. I could tell his brother had an eye for me, but all I wanted was Danny.

The friend ended up being an old sugar daddy when Danny was younger. After dinner, I started doing the dishes and Danny said he wanted to talk to his friend about something back in the bedroom. I admit being a little gullible at times, but really! I thought, surely, Danny wouldn't do anything like that. All of a sudden, though, we had more money.

Back on the road, we hooked up with a motorcycle gang. We spent the night out in the open. They knew all the spots to spend the night where no one cared. Danny came over to me after chatting for a while with the leader. They all kept cruising me and I was starting to feel like Faye Wray felt in King Kong when the natives were eying her for their big sacrifice, except I didn't have a ship to escape back to. Sure enough, Danny said, "its custom for the males to make it with the new chick in the group." I thought, what new chick in the group? We were just spending the night with them. Well, I wasn't in the mood to entertain Hell's Angels that night.

"But Danny," I cooed, "I love only you. I won't do it." The Angels didn't like that one bit. To this day, I feel Danny was trading me away to the natives so he could entertain their chicks for the night. I slept with one eye open all night. We were on our separate ways by the next morning.

We finally made it to Florida to visit Danny's mom. She was opening her own beauty shop on the Keys so she encouraged us to start beauty school. We did, but Danny said, "Let's register as brother and sister."

That numb and minty feeling was overcoming me again, so I said, "But Danny, why?"

"I'm A.W.O.L. and still legally married," he demanded. So, over night, I went from being 'married' to having a 'brother' I never knew I had. Looking back I really feel this was all so he could make it with half the other students, and he did!

After we had finished beauty school for the day, the students would hit the 'Happy Hour' bars. Danny would send me home after two drinks. But he stayed and partied for hours more. There were times when I would be home in bed and I could hear him and other women having sex in the other bedroom next to ours. I put up with it, hoping I would have him all to myself someday.

To save money while going to school, Danny used to follow milk trucks and swipe milk, eggs, and juice. I would turn tricks and would hitchhike along the Tammiami Trail to pick up some. That almost got me raped one evening, without pay, no less. The driver pulled into some woods and parked. "I've seen you hitchhiking a lot along here," he said. I was really getting scared by now because no one was around. I thought he might kill me afterwards.

As soon as he parked he started moving toward me. I jumped out of the car and ran back to the road. He scrambled after me but a car was coming and I stuck my thumb out and got a ride to safety. That was a real close one though.

One night in a lounge I met a John and he flashed a whole wad of money in front of me. "All of this is yours if you come to my house," he said. Was he ever rich? Danny's family couldn't wait to open all that money!

Another time I was talking with a trick a little too much. He worked in clubs up north and was on vacation in Florida. We discovered that we both knew a trans-gender that worked in Chicago. Well, he picked up on me by then and yelled, "Are you one of them too?" I had already received the money so I bolted out the door. He ran after me, tackled me in the street and shouted, "Don't ever fool me like that again," as he took his money back!

Three months into school the head of the business marched over to us and said, "Oh, Danny, there's someone here to see you in the office," as she pointed that way. The next thing we saw was Danny being hustled out of there by the military police for being A.W.O.L.! He told me later that they were moving him to Fort Dix, New Jersey.

We had a car by then, so I dropped out of school and drove up the interstate to be with him. Yes, I was a beauty school dropout (shades of Grease)! I flew up the highway at a hundred miles per hour, and only stopped for gas and bathroom breaks. I couldn't stand the thought of not being with my love and what they might be doing to him. Back then the speed limit was 75, and some states like Tennessee just said *Drive Safely* on their speed limit signs. Okay, I was a little over the limit on the east coast, I admit. As a matter of fact, I beat him there and he flew! He asked me when I met with him if I drove the car or flew, and couldn't believe I drove there so fast and didn't get a ticket!

While he served his time and settled things, I worked as a cocktail waitress off base. I had plenty of offers from our boys in the military, but I remained faithful to Danny. When he finally got out we went to see my folks for the first time since I had left home, and for Danny to meet them.

8

Mother hugged me and was very cordial to Danny, even hugging him too! Immediately she spotted that Danny had parked the wrong way on the opposite side of the street. "You can't park that way down here in Memphis," she started, "I don't know how they park up north, but you can't do that here! You'll get a ticket!" I never, ever even saw a police car on our street.

She must have been having a flashback of when I started driving. She told me to take the wheel one day. Our car had a stick shift. Well, everything went real smooth until I had to shift and turn into the driveway at the same time. I landed in the neighbors' shrubs, inches from the house! "STOP! STOP!" yelled Mom. I did, and then she yelled again, "Get out! Get out!" She backed it up and parked it in our drive. When I asked her how I did, I didn't get one word from her. The next week I had a car that you didn't have to shift, and Daddy taught me after that!

She also treated me like a guest all my life. I declare at times it was like Mommy Dearest, a book written by Joan Crawford's adopted daughter. No wonder Sis and I left at 18! Daddy was just a bystander most of the time staying neutral. When Sis was 12, a wonderful neighbor and friend until this day, suggested that Sis start shaving her legs. Well, Mother stormed over there, when Sis mentioned it to her and cussed the neighbor out, up one side, and down the other! "I'm her mother, not you!" When I hit puberty, Mom suggested that I shave under my arms, for the smell. I guess she wanted to beat the neighbor before she told me. This brought on more of the 'I'm dreaming of being a girl' thoughts!

Mom was never able to have children of her own. I gave her a Mother's Day card one year that said, "You were my friend before you were my Mother." She flew into a rage and told me that she was the mother and I was the son! So much for the friendship thing.

"Come on out Daddy, we have visitors," she yelled back toward the bedroom. Daddy came out of the bedroom to meet us with a wry smile on his face. He was also cordial and acted as if nothing at all was different about me.

"Hi Butch! Glad to meet you Danny," he said. I hadn't told Danny that my nickname was Butch so he gave me a strange look. (Isn't that the name of a dog? Or maybe that's Spike. Hmm.... same difference though.) I asked Daddy if he noticed anything different about me. He said, "Your hair is longer."

"Is that all," I replied incredulously.

"Your cheeks are also a little fuller," as he pointed to his using both hands. Same neutral Dad, I thought.

Funny he should mention my hair first, which he never had much of, just a fringe from ear to ear. Mother always made me wear a crew cut, well, it was practically a crew cut anyway. When I started letting my hair get longer one time, imitating the Beatles, she said, "Time to get a haircut." I just got a trim and she was mad! She marched me right back in there and told them to go shorter. She must have thought people wouldn't notice that Daddy didn't have any hair if I didn't either.

Mother had a radical mastectomy on one of her breasts a few years before. So she took me back to the bedroom to show me where they cut the breast off and show me her implant cup in her bra.

I said afterwards, "Well, let me show you my implants." I started to raise my blouse and she stopped me.

"No, that's okay. Never mind." So much for the 'I'll show you mine if you show me yours.'

Reflecting more on Dad's neutrality, when I visited them later, after one of Mother's strokes, Dad asked me to get him something out of the chest of drawers. When I opened the drawer there were 20 cartons of Kool cigarettes! "What in the world are these Daddy? Shouldn't she quit smoking now after the stroke?"

"Well, hell," he said, "they were on sale and she's going to smoke them anyway." I thought to myself, there's nothing like saving a buck while you let her smoke herself to death!!

Mother would always have Dad on a diet for his high blood pressure. He would have sweets hidden in every nook and cranny around the house. Just call her Sherlock Holmes.

Of course, I think they were both trying to off me! When I would visit, I was always a guest and a garbage truck. It was always time to clean out the fridge, pantry, and house. "Use up the eggs, and that carton of milk in the back of the ice box. Finish off that bottle of catsup before you open the new one. Eat that cereal on the top shelf first," they would say. Well, when I would crack the eggs they were bone dry, the milk looked like cottage cheese and I had to add water to the catsup just so it would squeeze out! No telling how long the new bottle had been in the pantry either. I think the cereal had been there since I left home at 18. Just why on God's green earth all that rancid food had to pass through my body just to end up in the garbage, I'll never know.

Mom ordered every gadget they advertised on T.V. She either used them once or never at all. "Can you use this, Butch," she would ask me. Not knowing what it was, she explained to me, "This chops, dices, and shreds. It's really very handy in the kitchen," she said as she started demonstrating it. I felt like I was watching a T.V. commercial!

"Hmmm…," I said.

"Well, just take it. It may come in handy someday," she insisted. Now I know the real reason they wanted me to get married and have children. Just so I could pass all those worthless gadgets down to them! Somebody might get some use out of them someday.

Funny thing, though, Mother ended up disinheriting me. Yep! She left everything to one of her sisters. Of course, Pauline started working on her as soon as Dad died. Her husband had Alzheimer's disease. "I'm going to be in the poor house some day," she cried to Mom. One Christmas, Mom gave her some money and she thanked her over and over again. "I can really use this. I'm so thankful," she cooed. It worked. Of course, Pauline owned 3 properties and was a millionaire to boot. She gave me the boot too. Blood is thicker than water, isn't it? If Daddy knew Mother did that, he would be flipping and flopping in his grave. He couldn't stand Pauline!

At least I have all these useless gadgets, and I'm still alive after all that rancid food I ate. Say, did you know that all those Gingtzu knives really do stay sharp for 30 years! I don't have anyone to leave all those gadgets to though. Maybe they'll end up in the Smithsonian Institute someday. Mom always said we had so much to be thankful for. Hmm.... next.

Speaking of being thankful, Mother always taught us to say our prayers before bed. "Come on kids, its time for bed. Let's say our prayers," she said.

I jumped up, started dancing, and singing, "Now I lay me, down to sleep..." Well, that got my pants pulled down and just to show me how unholy that was, she grabbed that dirty old flyswatter (and I do mean dirty, with squashed flies all over it), and let me have it. My prayers were a little more subdued after that one. In fact all she had to do was say she was going to get the flyswatter for me to behave. Plus, she could just look over at it and that would do the job!

Whenever we had a problem to get solved, Mother would always say, "Don't worry. We'll get it worked out." Funny, it was always worked out the way she wanted it worked out.

I just couldn't score on the religious angle. Although after my adoption, we went to the same church that a famous Hollywood star went to at one time. She and Sis played on the church softball team. Mom and I used to laugh every time a ball was hit her way and it went right through her legs or right out of her mitt.

She was beautiful and finally won Model of the Year (Sigh....). Did you hear me let out that sigh? Okay, if that went past you, it's the same one that just played Martha Stewart on T.V. Now you get it, don't you?

Well, her winning the Model of the Year gave Mom a brainstorm for Sis to enter the Miss Memphis pageant. "Now," Mom told Sis, "don't put on too much makeup. Look natural; they'll love that much better than all that heavy makeup."

When the pageant officials saw her, they started screaming at her, saying, "Why don't you have any makeup on? You'll look all washed out under all the lights. What's the matter with you? Don't you know how to apply makeup?" They slapped plenty of makeup on her after that. Of course she sulked through the whole pageant, and didn't win either. No wonder she and Mom didn't hit it off together.

Back to our visit, Danny, Mother, Daddy and I sat down and started talking, and that was enough for Daddy. "I think I'll go back and lay down for awhile," he said. He never was one for me and Mother to start jawing as he called it, while he was watching T.V. or reading. "I'll let all of you jaw for awhile, see you later," he said.

Danny and I left the same day to go back to Florida. I worked as a barmaid. I'm not sure what Danny worked at. It was probably more trouble than you can imagine.

At Christmas, they sold out of all of the trees. Danny and his mother were just beside themselves because we couldn't have one (gee, it was Florida, nice and warm anyway. It didn't even feel like Christmas to me). Well, Danny started rushing around the house and garage for a few minutes. Then he said, "Come on Michelle, get in the car." I did, and we drove about two miles up the road, parked, and Danny jumped out of the car, opened the trunk, and took out a saw. He climbed up a pine tree in someone's front yard and started sawing away! He got a nice size tree out of that deal. The lady of the house was watching in horror with her hands on her face, mouth dropped open the whole time. When we walked in the house with the tree, his mom acted so pleased.

We picked up a female hitchhiker one day. I thought Danny was going to sprain his neck looking back, talking to her as we drove along. We let her off and he couldn't wait to get home and leave me as he rushed back out. I knew what was going on, but I couldn't prove it. I'd had enough of him and left.

The only problem was how to leave him. I packed 2 suitcases and snuck out when he was in the shower. I almost got away clean except the cord of the hair dryer was caught in the zipper of one of my suitcases and when I tore out of there it banged against the nightstand. I jerked it out of the suitcase and ran out of the house. I hid in a grove of trees all night watching Danny drive up and down the street looking for me. I was scared because he had hit me once before in the face. I just had to get away. I just couldn't take it anymore. He finally gave up and I hitch hiked back to Baltimore. What would I do now?? I was at such a loss. How could I continue on without my hairdryer?

9

When I finally called Sis and told her about the change she said, "You should have told me first before you did that, Butch!" (Why does everyone keep calling me that awful name, especially now?)

"It's Michelle now, Sis," I replied.

"Its wrong," she insisted and refused to see me ever again. I did call her quite a few times over the years, but to no avail. I was able to see my niece and nephews over the years when visiting my folks.

One year at Christmas, my folks sent the grandkids gifts, but not her. She marched them right up to the front door and made them give them all back! Sis's ex-husband got custody of them eventually, with the help of my parents no less. That finished that relationship off for good. She wouldn't even go to my dad's funeral, or later my mom's. How sad! At least they fed, clothed, and raised us for a while. Sis got disinherited by Mother later too.

Back in Baltimore, I finally had my first sexual experience with a woman! I know, I know! You're asking why did I wait until after the surgery and not before to have sex with a girl. Frankly, I just couldn't get it up! There are you happy now that I've revealed my last deep, dark secret to you? The neighbor boys weren't the only ones interested in me after school.

It was with my roommate, Kelly, one of the few girls working in the Inferno club. Its funny, she suggested I try it with a girl before going through with the surgery. I still couldn't wish it up though.

The reason this started was because Danny came back to town. He wanted me back. I wouldn't go for that. He didn't give up, so I set up a date with him at the apartment. Kelly came up with a brainstorm to time his arrival while we were making love. He deserved to be paid back she said. He couldn't believe it when he walked in and saw us. Wouldn't you know it, though, he tried to join in! Kelly refused, so that was the end of that, and a first rejection for Danny.

You know, maybe I did accidentally pay Danny back one time on my own in Florida. We were all at the beach, boating and water skiing. We took turns pulling each other. When I was pulling Danny, I looked back and he was gone, nowhere to be seen. Well, somehow his hand got caught on the rope and he was dragged on the bottom for several minutes. I finally realized he was down there visiting the catfish and stopped the boat. Was he ever mad! You don't really think I did that on purpose do you?

Well, all that extra curricular activity caught up with Danny one day. He came to Chicago when I was there and was just getting well from V.D. He had the nerve again to try to get back with me! That was another rejection for Danny. That was the last time I ever saw him. I can honestly say I've never had a venereal disease my whole life. I know that's hard to believe, but its true! Kelly and I always used protection! It worked for us both. Plus the majority of people in the profession keep themselves pretty clean.

Kelly and I booked club dates, around the country. We both were exotic dancers by now. "Michelle! Guess what? Our agent wants to book us in Texas in one of the clubs," Kelly said all excited.

"Really?"

"Yes, and you won't believe this one. We get to stay at a motel with a pool for free," she said.

"Wow, that does sound pretty great," I remarked.

We flew to Texas, took a cab to the address given us and dropped our jaws. The motel was overgrown with weeds and was falling apart. "Well," Kelly said, "at least there is water in the cement pond!" That wasn't in much better shape. We were also in the middle of nowhere.

Honey Sweet and the twin 48's, the owner of the club and motel, met us there (and those 48's were not guns). She had also been an exotic dancer all of her life and still looked pretty good.

"Welcome, girls, to my place," she said. "Follow me to your rooms." A couple of her boys followed her with our luggage. She introduced us to Peg, a trans-gender in progress.

"Howdy all!"

"Feel free to use the pool and make yourselves at home. I'll send my boys by to pick you up at 7:00 p.m.," Honey Sweet said.

They left and we settled in and unpacked. At lunchtime, Peg suggested we go get something to eat. Her car was dead as a doornail. The place had no phone, at least not one that worked anyway. How could we get something to eat before we went to work? Peg spotted an old swayback nag in the field next door. "If I could find some rope I could ride that horse and get us something," she said. We found some rope in the office. She chased and tried lassoing that horse for an hour. She finally won and off they trotted to the restaurant. We got some food anyway.

Honey Sweet never danced at her club. We wondered why not. We kept egging her on to do a number someday, and she wouldn't do it. She would always just tell us maybe someday. Finally she agreed to do a number. Then we found out the real reason she didn't dance anymore. Those 48's hung all the way down to her hips. She'd had so much silicone injections and implants that they fell as she got older. Come to think of it, that's where guns are worn anyway, on the hips (shades of Gunsmoke)!

Honey Sweet loved her pet monkey. She would sit, petting him and would pick fleas off of him. In turn the monkey would pick through her hair and look for fleas to pluck out. Occasionally, that pet monkey got mad at Honey and would bite her being all excited. And what would Honey do? She bit that monkey back just to show him!!

Peg made Honey Sweet a little sour when Honey paid for Peg's sex-change and she skipped out of town. The hunter got caught by the game that time.

Later on, after working there a few months, Kelly and I got fired. Yep, fired. Honey Sweet limited us to two drinks while working in the club. I think this was because we would get pretty high at times. Well, we asked a customer to go buy us a bottle of vodka and a bottle of whiskey. He did and we all sat in the booth in the corner and got dead drunk. I passed out for a while. Kelly woke me up and said it was time to do my show. I was still high and fell off the stage behind the bar onto the floor. I wasn't hurt, but Honey Sweet was furious!

"Just get out," she yelled. We agreed, as we were getting tired of the Shady Rest Motel anyway. Before leaving, I started to take down the black fluorescent light I had bought. One of the boys told me I couldn't take it that it was the bars.

"I sure can, I bought it," I yelled back as he continued to disagree and argue. By then it was out of the fixture anyway so I said, "okay, you can keep it," as I hit him over the head with it. It shattered into a million pieces.

There is a code in Texas, leave one club and you won't be hired by another one. They stuck to it too. We went to several other clubs and they said the word was around about us and apologized for not being able to hire us.

Finally, a lady owner of the last club we tried felt sorry for us. She said that if we could leave town for a couple of weeks she could hire us when we got back. We did just that. We visited Kelly's folks for a couple of weeks in Chicago. Part of this was just to show Honey Sweet that she didn't own all of Texas!

When we returned we rented an apartment, and guess what? It had a pool right outside of the front door, and it was clean. However, the apartment had cockroaches the size of mice. It was war! Those bugs got high on all that bug spray and chased us. We banged them with the broom. YUCK! Crunchy! They say everything in Texas is bigger than anywhere else.

Two of Honey Sweets boys, who were also brothers, felt a thriving toward Kelly and me. They started coming over for visits. Somehow it was all crossed up though. I really liked the one that was with Kelly and him me. Wes, who was with me, liked Kelly, and Kelly liked him. It must have been all that bug spray!

Wes cozied up to me one day. He really just wasn't my type, a friend more than anything. I think he was trying to make Kelly jealous. Eventually, Kelly and Wes started going together. She was 4 foot 10 inches and I do declare that I'm not sure how she entertained him, but she did!

Everyone in Texas carried guns. Finally we were heading back to Chicago, with Wes no less. When we landed at the airport they were spot-checking luggage and to my surprise they found a gun in my trunk. I told them it wasn't mine and I didn't even know how it got in there. They kept it and I found out later that Wes and Kelly put it in there. Wes was trying to slip it into Chicago, in my trunk! That's the power of love, I guess. With friends like that....

Wes turned possessive and abusive toward Kelly, and they ended the affair. I think she enjoyed getting men to fall in love with her and then dumping them. She had been on the streets since she was a teenager, running around with queens.

One night at a club on the north side, Kelly rushed up to me and said, "Come on, Miss Thing. Go into the bathroom with me." When we got inside, she told me to pee in a glass she was handing me. "Say what?"

"Just pee in the glass," she repeated. As I was peeing in it she told me she had a John in the booth that liked to drink women's urine. He was paying twenty dollars a glass and she and all the other girls were dry. "Come back to the booth with me, he's buying everybody drinks too," she said. I followed her.

"Here's some more, honey." She said

When he tasted my urine, he said, "Oh, no! That's not a woman's urine. That's a man's!" Kelly and I gave each other a very dumbfounded look (shades of Water World)!

When we were working in another club on the north side, a preacher would come in the club trying to convert all of us several nights a week. He was really working on Tashia, a transgender in progress. He had her in tears at times, making her feel so guilty! Tashia eventually ended up converting the preacher and they became eternal lovers! The lesson learned was to not preach in hell or you might end up in it!

Bob Crane, the actor on "Hogan's Heroes" came in the clubs. He sure loved the *night life*! What a sad ending he had to love life as much as he did!

Kelly liked to chat with a cop named Toni Spumoni. One day when he came over for a chat, a couple of friends had just pulled a job and stored all the hot stuff in our basement. He never found any of it. Kelly was sweating that one out. Toni would go out drinking to catch thugs, drug addicts and burglars. This way he would loosen them up before the bust. He would eat raw bacon so he wouldn't get drunk with them. All that raw bacon finally caught up with him in Europe, while he was on vacation though. He bit the final bullet and they had to fly his body home.

When my 9th grade school teacher came in a club one night he didn't recognize me. I guess not! I did recognize him though. I called him by name and told him he was my teacher in my 9th grade science class. He denied that I was in his class, because he said he knew all his students. I mentioned a few lessons that he taught us such as how we all eat unborn chickens when we eat eggs and how in some countries they eat cow's eyeballs. He looked so surprised as I told him that. I had to go and do my dance number, but when I came back he was gone! I freaked him out, didn't I? He's probably still thinking about that.

Some lady who lived in our twelve-story apartment building in Chicago jumped off the roof one day. I'm not sure what that has to do with anything, but I thought I'd throw it in. I guess she had had enough by then. Oh, now I know! Well, speaking of high rise buildings, the John Hancock in Chicago was one of the tallest in the world. Some man threw a woman out through the glass, which was triple paned glass at that. She had quite a fall too.

At the same time I was dating a man named Herb. Kelly called him 'Herbal Essence'. He lived on the 5th floor of an apartment building. I wasn't sure if he knew my story or not. I passed out on his living room couch one night and woke up naked in his bed the next morning. There's nothing like "agreeing" to make love with someone. The saying "don't start without me" has a ring to that one. At least he didn't throw me out the window afterwards.

All of a sudden Kelly was busy every night after work. "You sure must be up to a lot," I would tell her but she wouldn't say anything. After months of this, she told me to go over to the club owner's house after work. After stopping to get something to eat, I took a cab over. When I walked in, everyone of the dancers, the owner, and his brother were having a wild party! Kelly just started laughing. They entreated me to join in with them. I did so reluctantly. I really wasn't that comfortable with this. I know, I know. You're saying she should be used to all of this by now. I felt comfortable having girls as friends, not making love with a whole group. Plus, they all knew I was a gender-bender.

Something similar happened in Florida one time before. As usual, Kelly and I were there working. A man was buying her drinks and invited us over to a party on a Saturday night at his mansion on the beach. We went. Someone answered the bell and invited us in. Fifty or more people were lying on the floor making love! Candles were lit and on the tables, foot high cocaine was piled up and they were rolling joints out of the yellow pages. We couldn't believe it. We puffed and snorted, and then Kelly said lets go before this place gets busted. These people were rich, too!

Kelly was married to a Hispanic man from Acapulco, Mexico. Well, all of a sudden she had another brainstorm. "Let's take a bus from Chicago to Acapulco. It will be so much fun!" She wanted to settle things with her husband there.

She packed lunch for us for the first day. About six hours later a smell you can't even describe was all through the bus. Everyone was looking around asking what the heck that smell was. I finally asked her what she packed for lunch. "Just some sandwiches, chips, and hard boiled eggs."

"Well, lets get it out and eat, I'm hungry!" When we opened lunch up that rancid smell really filled the whole bus. She had peeled the eggs the night before and now they were ruined.

"I just thought it would be easier if they were already peeled," she sheepishly said. We pitched them out the window as everyone on the bus was laughing at us.

Coming around the mountains and seeing Acapulco at night was beautiful. All the lights were twinkling in the valley and hills below. After three days and three nights of bouncing around on the bus and sleeping in the aisle on the floor, with people stepping on you as they got on and off the bus, it was extra beautiful to be there.

We checked into a motel and she called her husband. He showed up with a friend who was a middleweight prizefighter. I didn't ask for this one. I was on vacation and didn't want a boyfriend. Well, he had the hots for me. Kelly said, "Why don't you carry on with him, Miss Thing?"

I told her, "First of all, he's not my taste, and second if he picks up on me, that I was a boy, he might punch us both out of Mexico."

"Oh, don't worry about that," she said.

Well, he chased me around the room, and then threw me on the bed. I threw him back away from me and ran out to the pool. He came outside and followed me around for the rest of the day. He finally gave up and left. Kelly and her husband finally divorced because he wanted her to move to Mexico with him and she wasn't about to live there!

Could I stop here a moment and confess something else at this point in my memories? I'm really ashamed to admit today that most of the men I had sex with didn't have a clue about my real story. I think it must have been an inner desire to get revenge on the whole male population for the abuse they gave me. To this day they probably still don't realize that they had sex with Michael and not Michelle. At the time it was thrilling for me to know that they had no idea that they were enjoying sex with a man but in their own minds were having sex with a woman. I really wasn't in my right mind, was I? And who said, "Hell hath no fury like a woman (or in this case a man) scorned!"?

My sincere apologies to all of you today! Well, you shouldn't have been in those bars anyway, cheating on your wives! P.S. Please don't come looking for me. I'm really sorry. I mean it. Next....

10

Back in Chicago, we started a club engagement on the north side. I started facial electrolysis to remove what little beard I had. I also legally changed my birth certificate from Michael to Michelle.

We started going to Kelly's parents' house for Sunday dinner. I met her brother Frank there. Then he started coming to the north side for visits. Romance blossomed and we were married on Halloween night at city hall, which should have been the warning sign I was looking for. Kelly married one of the club owner's brothers.

I would like to report to you that we all lived happily ever after like Snow White and the Seven Dwarfs, but I'm sure you've all heard of the Diane Warwick song "Déjà vu," or Murphy's Law, which is if something can, will, or possibly go wrong, it will. Take your pick, either one of these will do!

Frank had a hard time holding down jobs also. He was in some trouble when he was younger, but I thought all that was behind him. I should have suspected something was wrong when he started making prank calls to the fire and police stations. He expected me to bring home the bacon and plenty of it for his gambling habit. He favored Bruce Springsteen, the singer, and I was really wild about him. Frank had more feelings and compassion for me than Danny did. I think they both loved me, Frank more so than Danny. Oh, all right, I admit it. They were both pimps. I might as well face it. You had that one figured out anyway, didn't you?

Still, they would become jealous of me if I'd get too familiar with the Johns. They were afraid I might run off with one. I almost did at one time. My Sugar Daddy made plans to cruise the world with me. He had plenty of money too. His health was not that good, because he was an older man. He wheezed and huffed and puffed all the time. I thought he was having a heart attack one time. I just couldn't imagine being on the high seas and him dying with me. Can you imagine the headlines? I cancelled that trip and stopped seeing him also, because I didn't want murder on my resume too.

Frank came close to murder one day! He had befriended a man who happened to have been buying me drinks all night at the club. He and Frank were in some kind of a 'deal' together. Unknown to me they had an appointment.

I got home from the club and was lying on the couch when there was a knock on the door. We were all shocked when we all saw each other. Frank started arguing with the man about how he knew me and the man had thought he bought a date with me. It quickly escalated into a fight. They fought and wrestled out into the front yard. Frank had a knife. It got away from him and he told me to get it and use it on him. Well, like I said, no murder on my resume! So I started cutting his hair off with it. He finally ran away. Frank and Kelly didn't let me live that one down for a long time. They kept calling me the 'Hair murderer'! I can't imagine what the man's barber said.

We also tried the 'normal life' road once. We moved in with his parents on the south side of Chicago near Midway Airport. He painted houses and I was a cocktail waitress at a motel lounge. Frank was always jealous of anyone that showed interest in me. He would come into the lounge in the evening and watch everything going on. The owner, bartender, and busboys were all showing an interest in me so that job didn't last long either. The funny thing is that I just can't figure out how he could let me strip and hustle, but wouldn't let me have any friends. Although he always went out and partied, playing pool, drinking, and gambling.

In reality, all of my life I have been used, abused, and kicked around. I think once you are raised in an abusive atmosphere you start to seek out abusers your whole life. You look for abusive situations because that is the norm for you. The abusers also seek out the abused and like scenarios dominate the abused. Do we both enjoy it? To a degree we must, at least for awhile anyway. But I believe this scenario does carry through your whole life to some extent, no matter how wise and knowledgeable you have become. I have found that it even extends over into the animal world for me. Your pets will even try to dominate you. My birds have a way of telling me to whistle and sing for them. I think they would have me dance for them if I would. Boy, I must really be easy. Do you think they could be pimping me too?

I think the sex change was in a way a form of suicide in itself. I've certainly tried enough times after the Sleepeze incident to kill myself. In one instance, when I was with Kelly, I was falling for her in a weird sort of way and she could be a real Scarlet O'Hara at times too, just like my mother and sister. I am drawn to abusive women, I know.

Kelly and a policewoman were having an affair to remember. I guess I was a little jealous, so I decided to end it. I popped about 16 Seconal prescription sleeping pills, ran out of the apartment and down into the laundry room table. Next thing I knew, I awoke the next morning in my nightgown with people doing their laundry. Kelly looked everywhere for me. She was beside herself. By the way, that was the same apartment where she had another brainstorm. When we moved in we had curtains but no curtain rods, so she nailed the drapes to the wall. They looked pretty good, too. Of course, you couldn't draw them open.

The other time or should I say another time suicide was on my mind was when I turned on the gas oven, without lighting it. I laid my arms and head on the open oven door. I passed out from alcohol lying there like that. I woke up with just a headache from that one. There must have been too much fresh air in the room from the window being open.

The final time, which you already know didn't work since I'm writing this book, was when Frank and I had an argument at his parent's house. I took a whole bottle of aspirin! *I'll show them all*, I thought. Well, please don't ever think of trying that. I was so sick all I could do for two days was lie on the floor in the bathroom, arms and head in the toilet, throwing up the whole time. I wished I was dead. I still can't take aspirin to this day.

I must have subconsciously been trying to kill all of them too when I became the happy homemaker. Everyone was over for a roast dinner (my first one). After cooking it for 5 hours, uncovered in the oven, it could have been used for batting practice at Wrigley Field. The potatoes came out okay though, nice and lumpy just the way Frank liked them. I just couldn't figure out why the roast wasn't getting tender.

I wasn't the only crazy one though. Frank's mom went to the basement one day and shot herself in the chest. She said she just couldn't take it anymore. I guess not. Having a husband that drank and wouldn't work (she was the breadwinner), a criminal and pimp for a son, and a daughter that was a stripper and prostitute, and now a daughter-in-law that…well, you know all about her. She lived through it, bless her.

Frank even went into the garage one day, closed everything up and started the car engine. He came to his senses before it killed him, though. He kicked out some boards and rolled out into the fresh air (and it was not over the roast).

I had about had enough myself by that point. I decided to leave Frank. I knew he wouldn't go for that, so I planned to go as far away as I could get on the sneak.

I talked to Mae and she said, "Go to Hawaii. There's good work there, and I'll give you the names of some sugar daddies I know there." It was going to take some doing to pull this off.

I started holding money back and Frank noticed. He said, "You're not making much money, are you baby?" I would answer him saying, "It's just been sort of slow, babe." I lied to him.

I finally saved enough money for the fare to Hawaii. I booked a flight, packed my gowns and clothes, and slipped away one evening while Frank was out drinking and gambling. I won a bottle of Champaign in the flight, and drank the whole thing celebrating. I began roaming around the 747 and insisted on going up the stairs. They promptly escorted me back to my seat and guarded me the rest of the flight.

Getting off the plane, I yelled, "Free at last!" Hawaii was beautiful. Swimming in the ocean and lying on the beach was so much fun by Diamond Head. I made friends with Nina and a few other girls in the club. Nina was known for getting high. One day, a group of us hit the beach all day. Well, Nina passed out on her side for hours while we swam. Nina finally stood up after waking up. She looked like she was half White Man and half Indian. Why, all she needed was a torch and she could have been the Statue of Liberty for peace between the White and Indians!

Of course, I kept imagining shark fins swimming all around me. It was the same year that Jaws was released. We were on a sunami watch the whole time. Still, it felt so good to be free. No pimps, no problems, no cares. Just me! I'll be my own boss. It was just like The Mamas and The Papas song, "Go Where You Want to Go, Do What You Want to do." I know what you are thinking; this has to be too good to be true for her.

I was working at the club one evening and looked over in a booth, and there sat Frank! How did he find me, I thought? To this day, I'm still not sure how he did, unless he went around asking my friends if they knew where I went. The only one that knew was Mae. She could have told someone, or he may have been able to get it out of her somehow. It's a mystery to me to this day.

"Sit down, baby," he said with that twisted smile on his face.

"Okay, honey," I replied.

He asked, "What are you doing here?"

"I'm working," I said in a busted voice.

"No, why did you leave me?"

"I thought we needed a separation," I answered him.

"I don't," he answered back, putting a gun in my side. I know what you are thinking again, but no one could possibly make all this up!

I was really scared. Is he going to kill me? "I want you back," he said (shades of the Baptist Hospital Psychiatrist again). I did some fast-talking, "I'm not really gay. Uh...I mean, I'm not really leaving you, honey," I cooed.

"I know you're not," he said. For three more weeks until my contract was up at the club he stayed right with me with that gun. In the apartment he followed me to the bathroom because the front door was right next to it.

"Honey, you don't have to keep pointing that thing at me. You're scaring me, it might go off. I'm not going anywhere."

"I'm going to make sure of it, babe," he replied.

I just pictured me going to the bathroom, bolting out the front door, running down the hall and getting shot in the back trying to make my escape, naked.

He slept with that gun on the nightstand or under his pillow. I lay awake that night trying to figure out a way to escape. How could I? I was on an island in the middle of the Pacific Ocean. Where would I go?

It was finally time to fly back to Chicago, back to his parent's house. The message was clear. He would kill me if I ever tried to leave him again. His mother laughed when we walked into the house and said, "Well, you wanted him, now you've got him!"

"Yes I do," I replied. This was mother's revenge for stealing her son, especially by a gender-bender. Why didn't they blame Kelly?

11

Things settled down between us and our relationship started growing again. He finally stopped flashing that gun, although I knew he still had it. I decided it was time to see my parents again, with Frank. In fact, we had decided to move to Memphis. I knew that would go over like a load of bricks with Mother.

Everybody was cordial with the introductions. I really can't imagine what my poor parents were thinking by now. I guess they were just learning to accept things for what they were.

"You can't move back to Memphis the way you are ever again, Butch," Mother said very firmly! There's that name again, Butch, but I did warn Frank this time though. I knew it. Frank and I just looked at each other. We left for the motel later on and the next day went out and rented a furnished apartment. We never told them we were living right in the same city as them.

I started working and things were going good until Frank got heated up one night. He started speeding down Poplar Avenue at 100 miles per hour at one o'clock in the morning. Two policemen sitting in a doughnut shop jumped in their cars and took off after us in hot pursuit (shades of Bonnie and Clyde). We were given Breathalyzer tests. Frank failed but the police matron said, "She is not intoxicated, officer." I think that was the beginning of his downfall.

He had the nerve to pull a job in the same club I was working in. "Why did you do that, Frank," I asked.

"Well, it was an easy one. It was like it was just begging me to do it."

"Great balls of fire," I said! All of that and a few more jobs caught up with him and it was time for him to go to the slammer. I'm thankful that he didn't reveal his plans to me beforehand to get me involved. That was so loving of him, I think.

He spent two years in prison in Tennessee, and I moved back to Chicago to live with his parents. Kelly was still married living on the north side. I began dancing again at a club on the west side. I stuck with Frank while he was in prison, visiting quite often. I befriended a girl at the new club I was working in.

Sandra and I started to go to the Cubs baseball games. I hated sports when I was young. I always felt clumsy and was made fun of. Now I grew to really enjoy baseball. Of course, I was a girl now! It was from a different perspective. We would sit out in the hot sun and drink beer and relax. Sometimes, there's neither rhyme nor reason to life.

Sandra had the hots for one of the players. The team would tear out there after the game was over and we followed them. They would drive around trying to lose all the fans that would follow them. Then they would go to different sports bars and party. We'd find them though.

Sandra and I loved to shop and do things together. One day we took off for an amusement park on the north side of town. We had a great time all day. I was tired, so I asked Sandra to take the wheel as we went home. We ended up hitting a utility pole, landing the opposite way in a ditch. We weren't hurt, but the car was totaled! Maybe that was my final warning sign.

I asked her later, "Sandra, what happened on the road to cause the accident?"

She looked very embarrassed and finally admitted sheepishly, "I didn't have my contacts in my eyes!"

"Great day in the morning," I said! "Why did you take the wheel?" Talk about the blind leading the blind. It really has some meaning to it in this one.

I did get a nice, new, shiny car out of the deal, but Sandra and I drifted apart afterwards. Another girl in the club didn't like me. She was telling all the customers I was a boy. One night when I had a little too much to drink she brought me a cup of coffee to drink. She said to drink it, that it wasn't too hot. I started drinking it and it was scalding! We got in a knock down, drag out fight finally over that. She eventually quit.

I was 5' 10" tall. An agent for a production of Sugar Babies with Mickey Rooney came in looking for tall girls for the play. I'd like to tell you that was my big break, but I just can't. Yep! I turned it down. I felt Frank needed me for moral support; maybe I should have been seeing a psychiatrist all along. One girl did make it big though, "It's a bird. No, it's a plane. No, it's…" I'll leave that to your imagination now.

12

Frank was finally released from prison, and I knew I had to try to end our relationship again. This time he let me go. I believe it was because I stuck by him while he was in prison. I asked for a divorce, but he said he wanted an annulment. I agreed to it. We stayed friends and kept in touch with each other. He would come over to my apartment to help with things from time to time. He worked on a good education while in confinement. He was so smart I don't know why he took the criminal road. Later on, Frank and a friend were arrested for the shooting and wounding of a policeman. He got 12 years before chance of parole from that.

Well, you're really not going to believe this one. My parents encouraged me to go back to beauty school to become a cosmetologist and I did! At twenty-eight years old, I took a nine-month course, studied hard, and passed state boards with flying colors. Of course, a few friends and I partied a little bit along the way!

I finally felt I was starting to live a normal life, to a degree. The air was getting fresher, the light brighter. Still, something was missing. Sometimes you don't need a plane to fall out of the sky on you to tell you something. It could be a simple knock on the door, but everything has to be at the right time.

In 1980, I decided to return to Michael after I started a deep study of the Bible. I realized what I had done all my life was wrong in God's eyes, although it seemed right in my eyes at the time. Now, I won't judge anyone for what they have done, are doing now or will yet do, but I ask all of you to think very carefully if you take the irreversible step of trans-gender surgery. For that matter, anyone, male or female, that is thinking of doing anything whatsoever to any part of your bodies. Beauty is only skin deep. It's what is on the inside that really counts.

In retrospect, I have to admit it was harder to return to Michael than to become Michelle. Michelle was changing gradually. Michael had to change practically overnight. My faith in God eased the pain somewhat.

When I was younger, I used to say to God 'why wasn't I born normal like everyone else? Why me?!' I know a lot of teenage suicides are over just what I went through. Please don't do that if you are confused and contemplating this act. Learn from my example so you don't have to go through the school of hard knocks.

Everything in life is a love-hate relationship anyway: parents, siblings, friends, lovers, and yes, even God. I hated Michael and blamed him for everything that happened to me in life. I also blamed God. So, I killed Michael and started loving Michelle. I eventually had to kill Michelle and love Michael once again because I started loving God once again, too.

As a graceful butterfly is released from the cocoon, I released Michelle, because she wasn't the truth, and the truth is what will set you free. So why did I really return to Michael? Was it for God or was it really for myself? Was it for the soul in me that was dying? Or was it the sin and imperfection that was in my life for the first 29 years of it? Maybe I'd just had enough of the gender-bender lifestyle.

Peggy Lee sang "Is That All There is in Life." I found out there is much more to life. Someday God will work out all things for everyone. After all, all wounds heal with time. So, my friends, I'll let you be the judge as to why I returned to Michael.

You might ask me, do I regret what I did at 18 years old? Yes, but I've learned to live with it. In God's high plan for humans, maybe, just maybe, He is learning something about our love for Him by what we do with our lives.

I couldn't wait to call Mother and tell her I'd decided to return to Michael once again. I thought for certain that they would be so thrilled, but it was anything but thrilling! "Butch, you have to make up your mind on this. You can't keep going back and forth. Let me know what you finally decide," she yelled, and hung up the phone.

I should have known that was coming, though. I'm in, I'm out, I'm this, and I'm that. Hmmm, I guess she had adjusted to Michelle after all for the past 10 years. So much for Dr. Jekyll and Mr. Hyde. Michael was going to return with or without anybody's backing!

I went into the hospital for surgery to have my breast implants removed. They decided to give me a local anesthesia, so I was awake the whole time! I will never go through something like that while I'm awake ever again!

The doctors pushed, pulled, and tugged until I was screaming! They finally removed them, but the stretched skin still left me with small breasts. I also didn't have any testosterone in my body either. So I still have small breasts. I stopped taking female hormones several years before I decided to return to living as Michael because they were making me gain weight. When I was 18, I weighed 145 pounds. Between 21 and 28 years old, I was gaining about 5 pounds per year. I was so shocked because when I was 17, I used to take 'weight on' liquid. That's supposed to help you gain weight!

Dressing as a man again was really tough. Imagine if you are a woman, and you decided to start living as a man. You cut all of your long hair off and start wearing men's clothes. You go about your everyday life trying to convince everyone you are a man now. All the while, you have small breasts and a high voice, not to mention a woman's vagina!

For the past 25 years, I've listened to people call me both a sir and a ma'am. I got more ma'ams than sirs. I used to correct them but I stopped doing so. I finally realized that beauty is in the eye of the beholder!

I'm not sure if people think I'm trying to change into a woman or I'm a woman trying to become a man! Yes, it's hard, but we need to love and please God more than ourselves.

I'm forever grateful to the young lady I studied the Bible with. She not only helped me to get on the road to life, but also helped me return to Michael once again. I confided in her and also a few other close friends in the Christian congregation. They all accepted me unconditionally right away for who I was. And the whole congregation did also, even though I'm sure some thought me 'a little strange' at first. That's true Christianity! They all took me right under their wings, no questions asked! They are my spiritual family.

At the same time it was quite a learning experience again. A young man in the congregation and I went to the beach on vacation one time. He encouraged me to take off my shirt in the pool. "After all, you're a man," he said. Well, the hotel manager ran out to the pool area and screamed at me, "You can't go topless here!!! What do you think you are doing?" I grabbed my t-shirt and put it on as my friend and I went running out into the beach area, vowing never to do that again!

Frank's mom didn't mind. She wanted to buy my mink coat. She got something out of the deal with me and Frank after all. Picture her wearing her mink coat into the Western Electric plant where she worked. She wasn't even bothered by it either.

Kelly called over the years to keep our relationship open, but she and I eventually had to let each other go. Our lifestyles just didn't mesh. She stayed with the 'night life' and I stayed with the 'Bible life.' I still love her to this day, actually more than I do Frank. He called from prison many times and sent me what little money he made, however, we also parted ways.

I'm thankful to their parents for accepting me as a part of their family regardless of what I was. Life does go on though. Sowing those wild oats for ten years seems like a distant memory now, twenty five years later. But, I honestly and truly believe being a true Christian now is the better half of my life, not to mention the best way of life.

Epilogue

Dad died in 1987, Mom seven years later in 1994. I stood by my mom's side at Dad's funeral, as Michael their son. I visited them several times a year by myself since I returned to Michael in 1980. The twenty-five years since then hasn't been easy. I've stayed single and celibate all that time. The old looks, stares, chuckles, and jokes came back. I've learned to live with them though. It's okay! I've accepted things for the way they are. I am content with my life now.

Say! I told you I would tell you about that one time I returned to the Baptist Children's Home again, didn't I? May I tell you why now?

This one was harder than all the above changes in my life and still is. It happened in 1994 when I was leaving Memphis after my mother's funeral. For some reason, I decided to drive out there and face my past. It was Sunday morning, and I couldn't believe it! Everybody was at church. The door was unlocked at the building and I went in. A roast was cooking in the oven with all the trimmings. It smelled so good as I peeked into the oven. You're stalling, I told myself. I remembered all the times I would hang around the kitchen waiting for a handout. I left there and went into the family room where we all watched T.V. together in the evenings. I remembered the house Mothers liked Lawrence Welk.

I turned and glanced over at the stairs that went up to my bedroom where all the sexual abuse began. I didn't think I could go through with it, even now. I slowly took one step at a time. It seemed like I was in a time warp. Each step I took, I kept looking at that top of the stairs where that bedroom was, fearing it all the more. It seemed like an eternity ago since I was here. How could that room have so much control over me, even now at 43? Step by step I inched my way to the top. I stopped. Could I go on? I had to. I went down the hall a short distance and looked into it. It was smaller than I remembered. I was finally there, looking at the room where all the sexual abuse started, where repressed memory made inroads into my mind, where the mental and emotional problems grew. This room really was my King Kong. I had been sacrificed here so many times, but wait! Beauty escaped from the island and it was beauty that killed the beast! Beauty had survived, didn't she? The beast is the one that died…

Let me stop here for a moment and mention one last movie. Did you ever see Home Alone? The one where the little boy was so afraid of the monster furnace down in the basement, but he finally overcame his fears in life and one day he saw that the monster furnace was just a furnace after all.

Well, my monster bedroom was just a bedroom, after all, I discovered. I had made it after all these years, with scars, but I had finally made it!!! My 'monster' was finally dead. I turned and walked away, vowing never to return there ever again.

Disclaimer

I almost called this book "Michael's Revenge," but I thought better of it. There's a lot more stories in "The Naked City" I could share with you, but this could go on forever.

Now, don't you think this book was a lot more juicy and exciting than Hillary's book? Come on, admit it...

Back to the disclaimer, everybody in this book is either dead, still high, crazy, insane, or just plain doesn't care anymore. However, I have changed the names to protect the innocent, uh, I mean the guilty.

P.S. A big thanks to all my friends and associates for accepting me for whom and what I've really been over the years. It proves inner beauty is far more important than outward appearances. Anyone with any problems should sit down and write out their life's memories on paper. It's the best therapy yet!

Meditation

Can I truly say that this really does seem natural and it's the way we are supposed to live our lives? After all, most trans-genders are born physically in a certain way. Our minds may be different from our bodies, but which one should win over? Can we change our minds or change our bodies easier?

I feel if I had waited until I was twenty-nine to have the change I might not have decided to have the surgery. Everyone matures at a different rate. I've known some people who were in the hospital and ran out after changing their minds, while others threaten suicide to get the surgery! Are their deeper motives than just wanting to be the opposite sex? Maybe visiting a psychiatrist first is for the best, just to make sure.

Was I trying to hurt everyone that hurt me or that I love sub-consciously? Was I unworthy of being normal or maybe unworthy of life itself? I meditate on these things for my own sanity. I feel anyone alive would want to be normal and be a part of the normal society. I must admit, though, at fifty-five, it is easier to be living as Michael now than as Michael from age one to eighteen. Am I more mature, wiser, older, or just giving in to normalcy?

Life is short, but beautiful. We can't allow others to control our lives by what they do to us, robbing us of God's perfect gift to us. One day when we are all perfect, all the abuses and wrongs thrust upon us in our lives will be a distant fading memory like the setting sun, fading on the horizon after a sweltering hot day. Our minds will be at rest when that cool calm peaceful night comes, and it will last forever!!

The Bible says some men are born eunuchs, others are made eunuchs by men, and some men make themselves eunuchs. Scientists now claim it is genetic. I'm not sure if what I've been through is in my genes or not. I do believe, however, that the sexual abuse and my uncontrolled desires of youth drove me in that direction.

So, I was really made a eunuch by both men and myself, particularly at the surgical stage. Whether I was influenced by my genes or not, God can determine and He will settle that issue in time.

I do know that I am able to control my desires to an extent now. Yes, those feelings do crop up from time to time, but I don't have the burning desire anymore to fulfill them. I am truly at peace with myself now.

The Bible also mentions prostitution, immorality, and sin throughout its pages. Even the best of God's servants fell into sin, such as David, Solomon, and many of his other people of old. Still others practiced these things but stopped when they found the truth of the Bible which says, "Yet that is what some of you were. But, you have been washed clean, but you have been sanctified, but you have been declared righteous in the name of our Lord Jesus Christ and with the spirit of our God" (I Corinthians 5:9–11).

So I can and do have a clean conscience from all my past immoral sins. This enables me to live the "good life, now and forever!" So may all of you too!

Afterthoughts

The surgery on the lower half is irreversible; at least it was in 1980. Although some are telling me recently they are performing 'female to male' surgery. Just call me Mike the Dyke. I'll have to think about that for a long time. I do hear though they do it by taking a rib from the chest and transplanting it in that area!

That sounds kind of like what happened in the Garden of Eden, doesn't it? Adam gave up one of his ribs for Eve to be created. HMMM...I don't know. Plus I always thought ribs were for barbequing anyway. I'll still think about it, though. If I do decide on that, I'll let you know in another book. Of course, all four of my parents would roll over in their graves, and I'd really need a good psychologist by then. I'd love to hear from some of you and get your ideas on that one.

Final Thought

(I absolutely mean it!)

I've definitely decided against the rib thing. No, it's not the money. Hopefully I'll make something on this book. It's because I know everybody would just love to start calling me Butch again! I really don't think I could take that one again. Ever!

Poem

What am I anyway?
Do I stay or return right away?

Does it really matter what they say?
I'm still just me, don't you see?

So, can I please anyone today?
Only if you're far, far away…

I'll just have to say goodbye,
Or will I somehow simply die.

Please accept me for what I am…
And we will call a truce

If not, I don't know how I'll cope,
And I just might come loose.

And that would simply be abuse
For me and also for you.

If we look to happier days,
What will we do and what will we say?

That you and me can live our lives
Inside us until we die.

Also it has to be without the lie!!
Otherwise, we would probably cry.

All at once I know it's time
To up and go, so that's just fine.

Don't you see, don't you see?
That it's only really me!

I'm returning for all to see,
So don't judge me and I won't judge thee.

Yes, we've all made mistakes,
But they will only make us great!

We will all make it somehow
When we're perfect, holy cow!

Our heart, mind, body, and soul
Will always keep us truly whole.

This is the whole obligation of man,
To see us live together again.

Wake up, wake up, can't you see?
I'm once again just plain me!

Playing with my adoptive mom's jewelry

Sis and me at the zoo

Sis's sewing machine

My male doll

My arm after the Bel-Air car wash accident

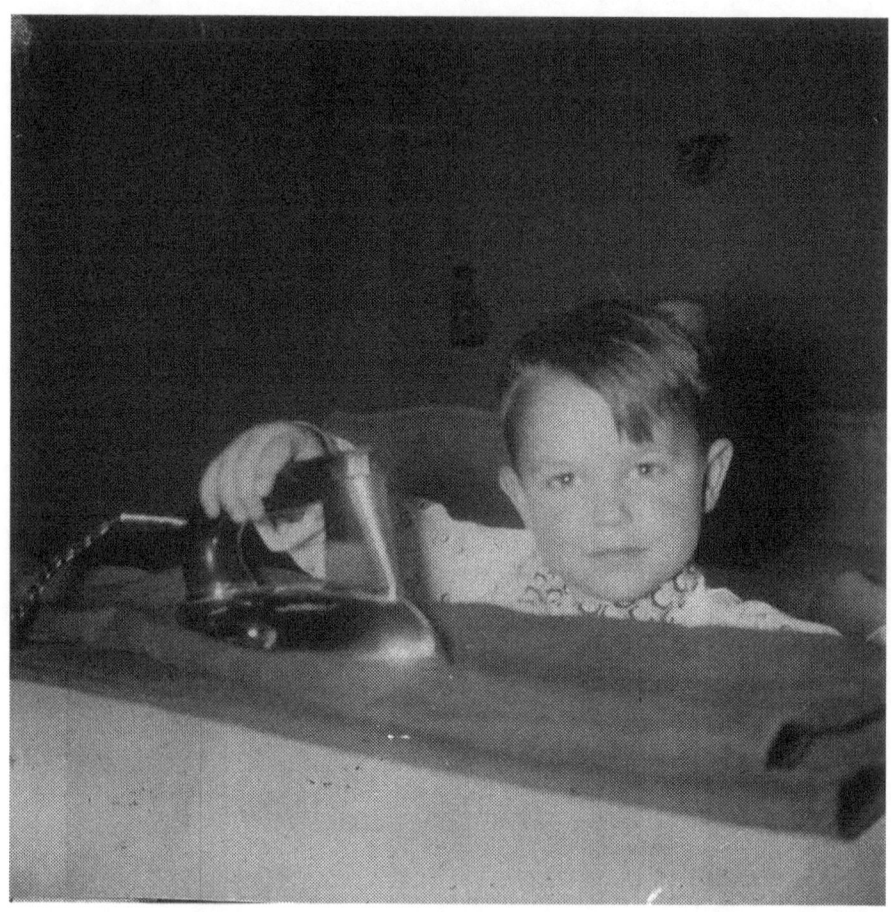

Mom's little helper

Summer fun in the backyard

Going to church

Our little beagles

Sis and a beagle pup

My older bedroom

In front of our new home

Our family room

Going to a costume party

Swimming at Reelfoot Lake

My puppy friend

School days

One of our baby chicks

Annie our Beagle

Fun at the ocean

Sis having fun

Dressing Annie up

Our motel on the beach

Another puppy

More pups

Cub scouts

Boy scouts

A foot of snow

In scouts

Cindy our other beagle

Fishing on the lake

Opening gifts

Cooking

My adoptive mom

My adoptive dad

Acapulco

Acapulco

Adoptive folks

WILL THEY SEE SANTA?—It's up to you. On Dec. 7, Memphis and East Memphis Exchange Clubs will sell that day's issues of The Press-Scimitar. Money raised from those sales go to support many worthy projects each year—including St. Peter's Orphanage, Porter-Leath Home and Baptist Children's Home. Three reasons why you should buy your Dec. 7 Press-Scimitar from an Exchangeite are these three, for whom Exchange can make Christmas a wonderful, gift-filled day. Left to right: Brenda, 2, St. Peter's, Butch, 4, Baptist Home, and Barbara, 6, Porter-Leath.

In the paper

OUR CHILDREN

And

OUR CHILDREN'S HOMES

1956

Four Homes For Children

"Then were there brought unto Him little children."
—Matthew 19:13

Michael at age 17

978-0-595-39969-7
0-595-39969-X

www.ingramcontent.com/pod-product-compliance
Lightning Source LLC
Chambersburg PA
CBHW051449280526
45785CB00003B/1491